THE LIBRARY OF
PIANO
PRAISE

To Richard Coolidge, for shining the light

EDITOR: AMY APPLEBY
EDITORIAL ASSISTANT: ELAINE ADAM
MUSIC RESTORATION AND ENGRAVING: ANNE DENVIR

ORDER NO. AM 980650
US INTERNATIONAL STANDARD BOOK NUMBER: 0.8256.2962.4
UK INTERNATIONAL STANDARD BOOK NUMBER: 1.84449.630.9

EXCLUSIVE DISTRIBUTORS:
MUSIC SALES CORPORATION
257 PARK AVENUE SOUTH, NEW YORK, NY 10010 USA
MUSIC SALES LIMITED
8/9 FRITH STREET, LONDON W1D 3JB ENGLAND
MUSIC SALES PTY. LIMITED
120 ROTHSCHILD STREET, ROSEBERY, SYDNEY, NSW 2018, AUSTRALIA

PRINTED IN THE UNITED STATES OF AMERICA BY
VICKS LITHOGRAPH AND PRINTING CORPORATION

AMSCO PUBLICATIONS
A PART OF THE MUSIC SALES GROUP
NEW YORK/LONDON/PARIS/SYDNEY/COPENHAGEN/BERLIN/TOKYO/MADRID

Contents

Art Thou with Me?

Johann Sebastian Bach
(1685–1750)

Andante

Ave Maria

Johann Sebastian Bach
(1685–1750)

Melody by Charles François Gounod
(1818–1893)

Andante cantabile

9

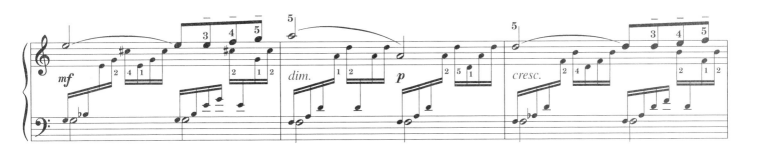

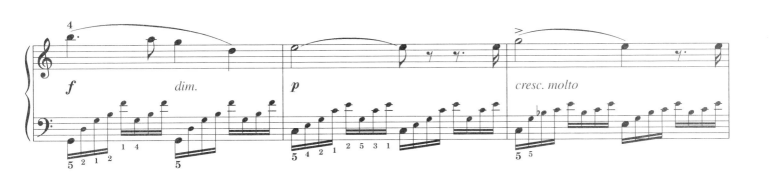

Chorale

Johann Sebastian Bach
(1685–1750)

Maestoso

Chorale

Johann Sebastian Bach
(1685–1750)

O Blessed the House, Whate'er Befall

Johann Sebastian Bach
(1685–1750)

Moderato

Jesu, Joy of Man's Desiring

Johann Sebastian Bach
(1685–1750)

My Heart Ever Faithful

Johann Sebastian Bach
(1685–1750)

Moderato

with Pedal

Prepare Thyself, Zion

from *Christmas Oratorio*

Johann Sebastian Bach
(1685–1750)

Allegretto grazioso

Prelude in F Major

Johann Sebastian Bach
(1685–1750)

Allegretto

Prelude in G Major

Johann Sebastian Bach
(1685–1750)

Grave

with Pedal

Allegro

Sheep May Safely Graze

Johann Sebastian Bach
(1685–1750)

Sleepers Awake

Johann Sebastian Bach
(1685–1750)

Moderato tranquillo

Now the Day Is Over

Joseph Barnby
(1838–1896)

Quietly

with Pedal

Pilgrim's Song of Hope

Antoine Eduard Batiste
(1820–1876)

INTRODUCTION

Agnus Dei

Ludwig van Beethoven
(1770–1827)

Adagio ma non troppo

Ode to Joy

Ludwig van Beethoven
(1770–1827)

Moderato

with Pedal

God, Thy Great Goodness Never Ends

Offertory

Ludwig van Beethoven
(1770–1827)

Andante

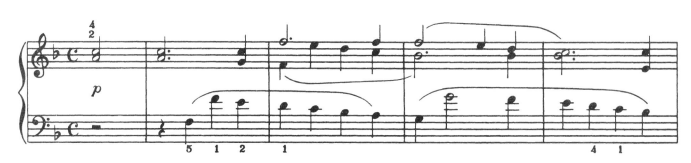

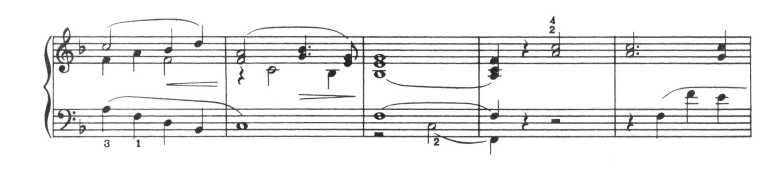

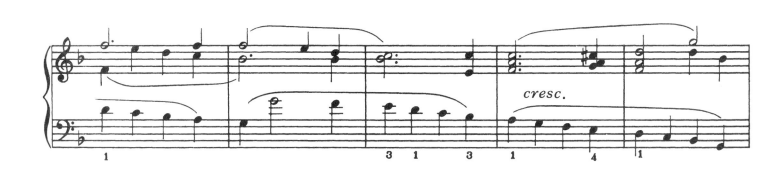

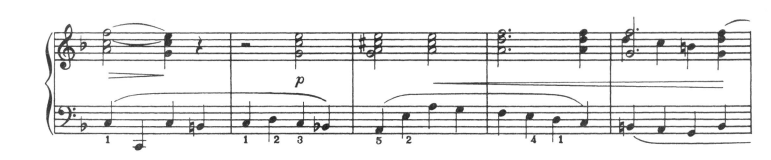

The Glory of God in Nature

Ludwig van Beethoven
(1770–1827)

Maestoso

Prayer

Ludwig van Beethoven
(1770–1827)

Maestoso

Theme and Variations on a Patriotic Anthem

(God Save the King—My Country 'Tis of Thee)

Ludwig van Beethoven
(1770–1827)

Maestoso

Theme

Var. I.

Var. II.

52

Var. III.

Agnus Dei

Georges Bizet
(1838–1875)

Maestoso

Allegro moderato

Processional

from *The Liturgical Service for the Organ*

Alexandre Boëly
(1785–1858)

Moderato

Offertory

from *The Liturgical Service for the Organ*

Alexandre Boëly
(1785–1858)

Moderato

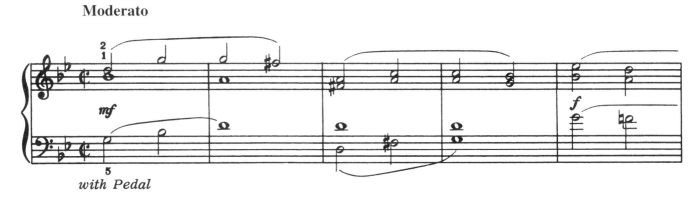

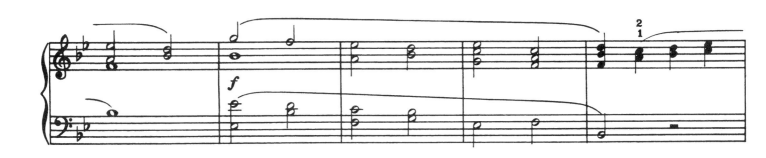

Postlude

from *The Liturgical Service for the Organ*

Alexandre Boëly
(1785–1858)

Moderato

with Pedal

Andante Religioso

Alexander Borodin
(1833–1887)

With a steady beat

64

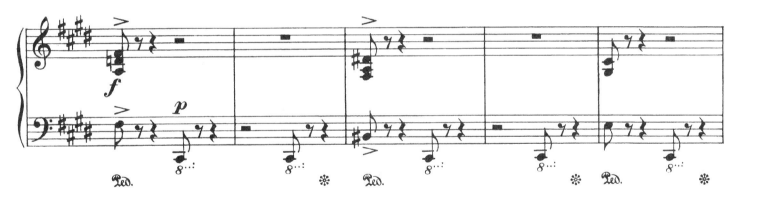

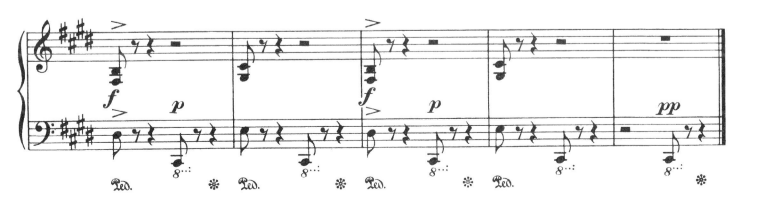

Angel's Serenade

Gaetano Braga
(1829–1907)

Andante con moto

Saint Anthony Chorale

from *Variations on a Theme of Haydn*

Johannes Brahms
(1833–1897)

Prelude

Op. 28, No. 20

Frédéric Chopin
(1810–1849)

Postlude in C

Op. 28, No. 8

Christian Cappelen
(1845–1916)

Energico

with Pedal

Funeral March

from *Sonata Op. 35*

Frédéric Chopin
(1810–1849)

Lento

The Prince of Denmark's March

from *Choice Lessons for the Harpsichord or Spinet*

Jeramiah Clarke
(1674–1707)

Andante maestoso

The Palms

Jean Baptiste Fauré
(1830–1914)

Andante maestoso

Christmas Carol

César Auguste Franck
(1822–1890)

Panis Angelicus

César Auguste Franck
(1822–1890)

Lento

with Pedal

Marche Pontificale

Charles François Gounod
(1818–1893)

Allegretto maestoso

O Savior, Hear Me

Christoph Willibald von Gluck
(1714–1787)

Andante

with Pedal

Arietta

Op. 12, No. 1

Edvard Grieg
(1843–1907)

Poco andante e sostenuto

Bell Ringing

Op. 54, No. 6

Edvard Grieg
(1843–1907)

Hallelujah Chorus

from *Messiah*

George Frederick Handel
(1685–1759)

Allegretto moderato

He Shall Feed His Flock

from *Messiah*

George Frederick Handel
(1685–1759)

Larghetto

with Pedal

Largo

from *Xerxes*

George Frederick Handel
(1685–1759)

Larghetto

March

from *Saul*

George Frederick Handel
(1685–1759)

Grave

Con Ped. sempre

See the Conquering Hero Comes

from *Judas Maccabeus*

George Frederick Handel
(1685–1759)

Moderato

con Ped.

Solemn March

from *Joshua*

George Frederick Handel
(1685–1759)

Postlude

Franz Joseph Haydn
(1732–1809)

Jesus Shall Reign

John Hatton
(1809–1886)

Maestoso

with Pedal

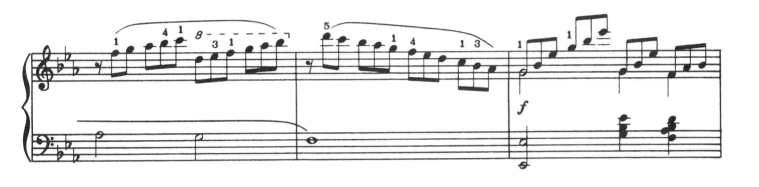

Ave Verum

Franz Joseph Haydn
(1732–1809)

The Heavens Are Telling

from *The Creation*

Franz Joseph Haydn
(1732–1809)

Grave e Cantabile

from *The Seven Last Words*

Franz Joseph Haydn
(1732–1809)

Grave e cantabile

With Verdure Clad

from *The Creation*

Franz Joseph Haydn
(1732–1809)

Andante

Prelude

Johann Michael Haydn
(1737–1806)

Grave

with Pedal

Evening Prayer

from *Hansel and Gretel*

Engelbert Humperdinck
(1854–1921)

Moderato

Shepherd's Sunday Song

Conradin Kreutzer
(1780–1849)

Maestoso

Prayer

Conradin Kreutzer
(1780–1849)

All Around Is Silence and Peace

Offertory

Friedrich Kuhlau
(1786–1832)

Lento

with Pedal

Monastery Bells

Louis Alfred Lefébure-Wély
(1817–1869)

Andantino

132

Ave Maria

Franz Liszt
(1811–1886)

Offertory

Edward MacDowell
(1861–1908)

Allegro moderato

A Mighty Fortress Is Our God

Martin Luther
(1483–1546)

Maestoso

The Last Dream of the Virgin

Jules Massenet
(1842–1912)

Andante religioso

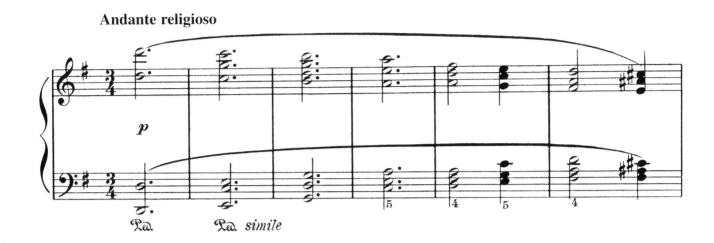

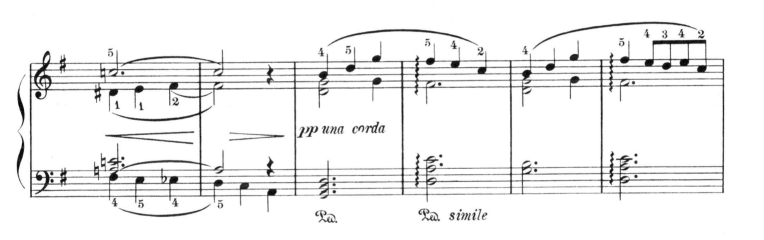

142

The Angelus

from *Picturesque Scenes*

Jules Massenet
(1842–1912)

But the Lord Is Mindful

from *St. Paul*

Felix Mendelssohn
(1809–1847)

Andantino

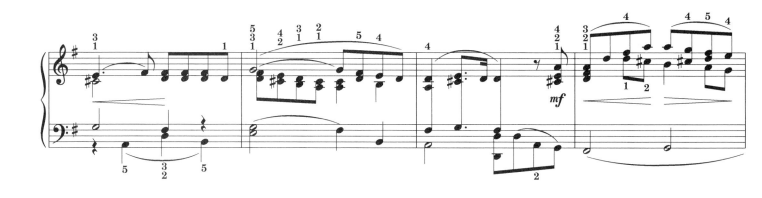

I Waited for the Lord

from *Hymn of Praise*

Felix Mendelssohn
(1809–1847)

151

O for the Wings of a Dove

from *Hear My Prayer*

Felix Mendelssohn
(1809–1847)

Moderato

O Rest in the Lord

from *Elijah*

Felix Mendelssohn
(1809–1847)

Andantino

Wedding March

from *A Midsummer Night's Dream*

Felix Mendelssohn
(1809–1847)

Allegro vivace

Coronation March

from *Le Prophète*

Giacomo Meyerbeer
(1791–1864)

Maestoso

Funeral March

Wolfgang Amadeus Mozart
(1756–1791)

Adagio

Agnus Dei

Wolfgang Amadeus Mozart
(1756–1791)

172

Ave Verum

Wolfgang Amadeus Mozart
(1756–1791)

Andante sostenuto

Kyrie Eleison

Wolfgang Amadeus Mozart
(1756–1791)

Lacrimosa

Wolfgang Amadeus Mozart
(1756–1791)

Sanctus

Finale

Wolfgang Amadeus Mozart
(1756–1791)

Moderato

March of the Priests

from *The Magic Flute*

Wolfgang Amadeus Mozart
(1756–1791)

Trumpet Tune

Recessional

Henry Purcell
(1659–1695)

Moderato maestoso

Cujus Animam

from *Stabat Mater*

Gioacchino Antonio Rossini
(1792–1868)

Siciliano

Offertory

Domenico Scarlatti
(1685–1757)

Moderato

p   grazioso

Ave Maria

Franz Schubert
(1797–1828)

Lento

Unfinished Symphony

Theme

Franz Schubert
(1797–1828)

Allegro moderato

Remembrance

Robert Schumann
(1810–1856)

Espressivo

Swedish Wedding March

August Söderman
(1832–1876)

Allegro e leggiero

194

God So Loved the World

John Stainer
(1840–1901)

Moderato

with Pedal

Church Air

Alessandro Stradella
(c.1645–1682)

The Lost Chord

Arthur Sullivan
(1842–1900)

Moderato

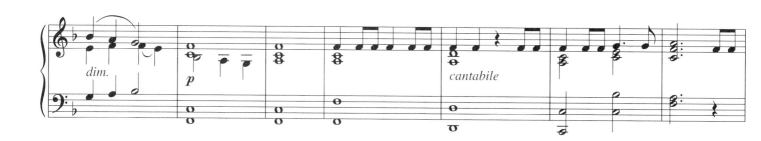

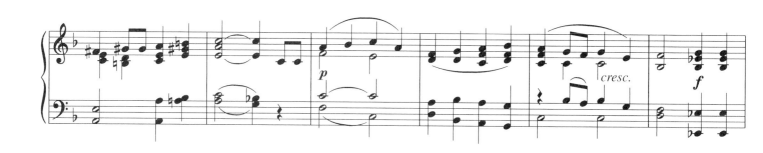

Andante Cantabile

from *Symphony No. 5*

Peter Ilyich Tchaikovsky
(1840–1893)

Con espressione

with Pedal

204

205

In Church

Peter Ilyich Tchaikovsky
(1840–1893)

Moderato

Morning Prayer

Peter Ilyich Tchaikovsky
(1840–1893)

Lento

Glory Be to God on High

Georg Philipp Telemann
(1681–1767)

Maestoso

Andante Religioso

Francis Thomé
(1850–1909)

Con espressione

Old Welsh Carol

Traditional Welsh carol

Andantino

Amazing Grace

Traditional Scottish air

Majestically

with Pedal

What Child Is This?

Traditional English carol

Quietly

mp

with Pedal

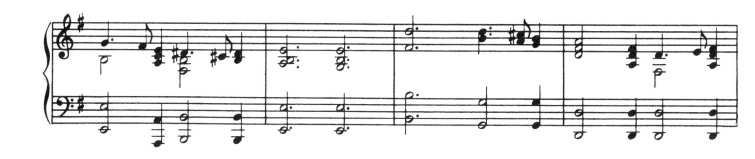

Sicilienne

Offertory

Daniel Gottlob Türk
(1750–1813)

Andante

with Pedal

Adeste Fideles

Paraphrase

Renaud de Vilbac
(1829–1884)

Andante

Postlude

Robert Volkmann
(1815–1883)

Allegro moderato

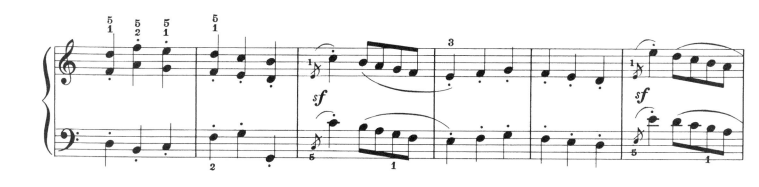

Bridal Chorus

from *Lohengrin*

Richard Wagner
(1813–1883)

Con moto moderato

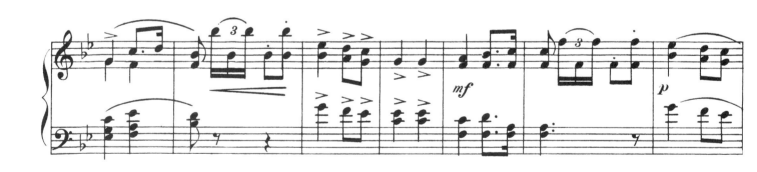

Prayer

Carl Maria von Weber
(1786–1826)

Adagio

Siciliano

from *Sonata for Violin and Piano in A Minor*

Carl Maria von Weber
(1786–1826)

Allegretto

Pleyel's Hymn

William Westbrook
(1831–1894)

Shepherd Boy

Grenville Dean Wilson
(1833–1897)

Love Divine

John Zundel
(1815–1882)

Moderato

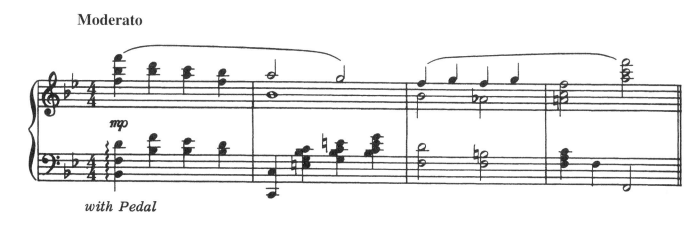

Index